Adult Coloring Book

Stress Relieving Stunning Designs

Bundle of over 120 Unique Designs

Pat Woods

Thanks for purchasing Pat Woods's Adult Coloring Book: Stress

Relieving Stunning Designs

We recommend you also to get her other books:

Adult Coloring Book: Amazing Designs

You can purchase it on this Link:

https://www.amazon.com/dp/1717999263

Adult Coloring Book: Stress Relieving Mandala Designs

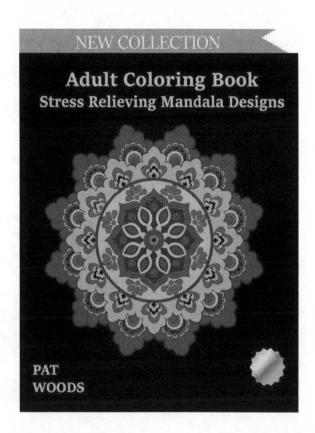

You can purchase it on this Link:

https://www.amazon.com/dp/1717758916

Adult Coloring Book: Stress Relieving Unicorn Designs

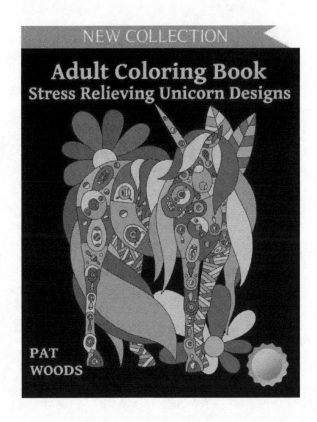

You can purchase it on this Link:

https://www.amazon.com/dp/1718025513

Adult Coloring Help Relieve Stress and Anxiety

There has been a huge wave about adult coloring books. Coloring books are no longer just for children. It is now advocated by therapists, psychologists, healers and alternative medicine practitioners as an effective form of fighting off stress. It is even advocated as an alternative to meditation.

The American Art Therapy Association has even done a study on "Art Therapy" which includes adult coloring books. It is incredible how powerful an adult coloring book can be.

It can reduce stress, bring self-awareness, increase self-esteem, develop social skills, improve your sense of reality, reduce anxiety and panic. Not to mention the creative benefits of it, as a means of self-expression, a fantastic creative outlet.

It also brings about mindfulness. There is a lot of tranquility in coloring an image.

We recommend you do not use crayons but coloring pencils for more precision and relaxation.

Enjoy this coloring book and take your time! ☺

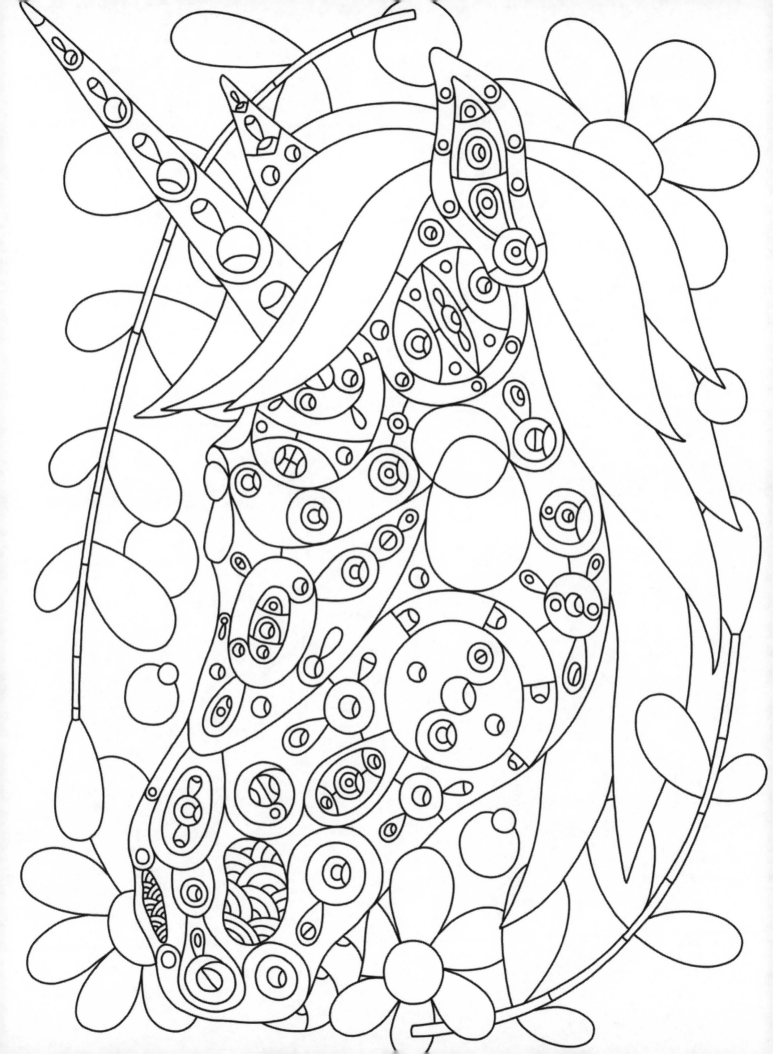

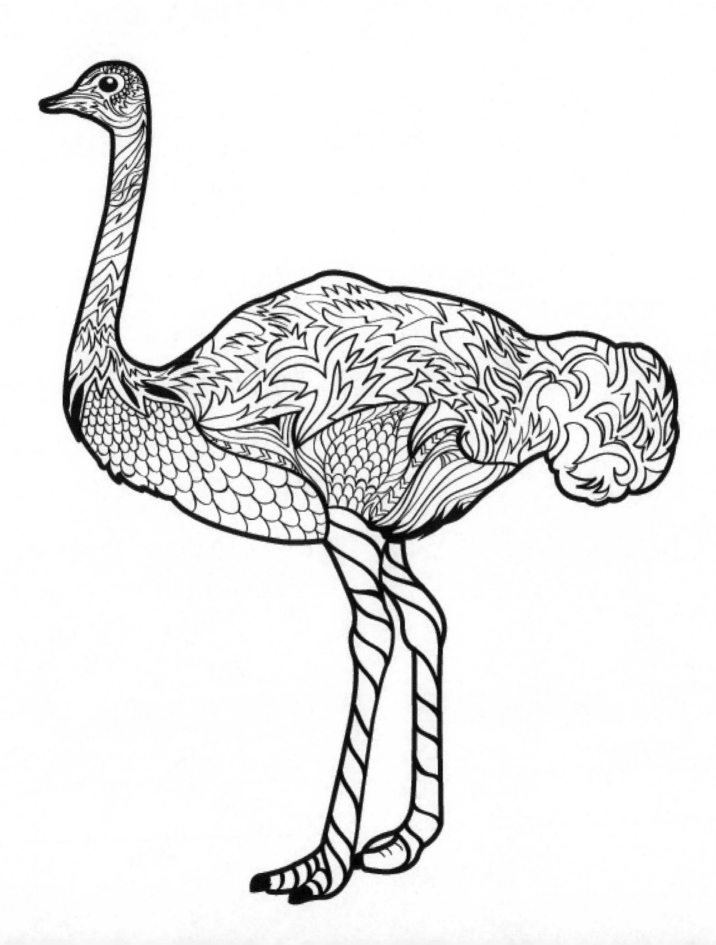

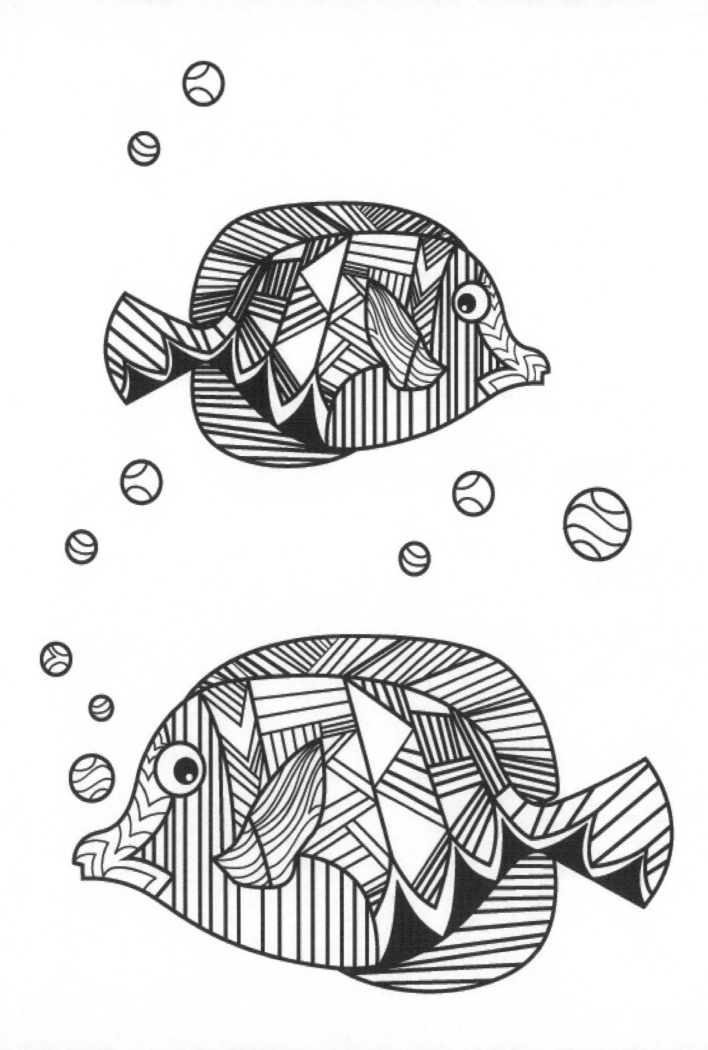

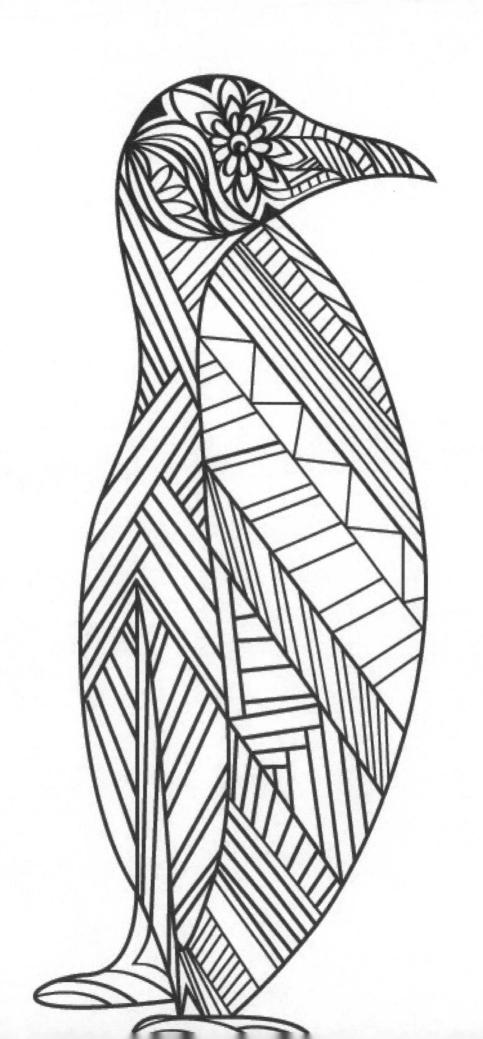

Roses

Thank You!

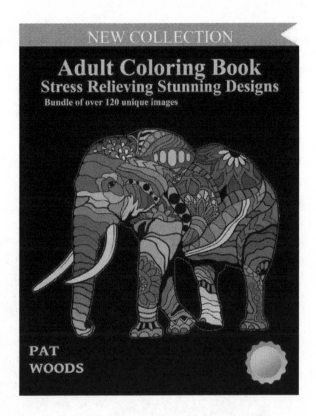

Thank you for purchasing my book.

I hope that the Adult Coloring Book made you feel relaxed and calm and that you enjoyed the journey of your inner exploration.

Practice coloring into your daily life for a Peaceful, Positive Mind.

Thanks for purchasing Pat Woods's Adult Coloring Book: Stress

Relieving Animal Designs.

We recommend you also to get her other books:

Adult Coloring Book: Amazing Designs

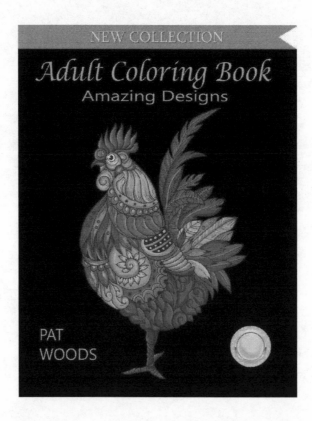

You can purchase it on this Link:

https://www.amazon.com/dp/1717999263

Adult Coloring Book: Stress Relieving Mandala Designs

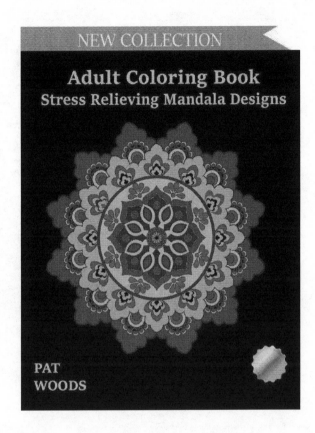

You can purchase it on this Link:

https://www.amazon.com/dp/1717758916

Stress Relieving Fascinating Designs

You can purchase it on this Link:

https://www.amazon.com/dp/1720125236

Made in the USA
San Bernardino, CA
06 April 2019